Keeping it weird

Poems & Stories
of Portland, Oregon

Keeping It Weird

Poems & Stories of Portland, Oregon

Editing & Book Layout:
Shawn Aveningo

Cover Design & Photography:
Robert R. Sanders

Library of Congress Control Number: 2014915762

ISBN-13: 978-0692248416
ISBN-10: 0692248412

Published by The Poetry Box™, 2014
Beaverton, Oregon
www.ThePoetryBox.com
530.409.0721

This Wonderfully Weird
Collection of Poetry & Stories
is dedicated to
all the inhabitants of Portland
and anyone who seeks
to find beauty in the weird,
and oftentimes wet.

Table of Contents

In January 2014, *The Poetry Box*™ relocated to Portland, Oregon – land of all things weird – at least, that's what we were told. Everywhere we turned, we saw billboards preaching "Keep Portland Weird" or bumper stickers touting "Weird Is Where It's At." Now, don't get me wrong; we LOVE Portland, and we were diligent in our preparation for the new locale.

We religiously watched each season of *Grimm,* putting Nick and Monroe in our contact list just in case we encountered any strange *Wesen* creatures. We binge-watched *Portlandia* to learn how to recycle our toothpicks and of course "Put a Bird On It", which inspired our weirdly whimsical Call for Submissions flyers. We even devoured dozens of *Voodoo Donuts* to hold head-to-head taste battles with *Blue Star.*

Now that we've been here almost a year, we have witnessed so much more about this delicious melting pot of human creativity and sustainability. And thanks to our wonderfully weird contributors, we are able to share the unique, quirky, sometimes bizarre and oftentimes wet tales of this town known as Portland, Oregon (aka. Rip City, Stumptown, Rose City, Bridge City, P-Town)

Embrace the lively literary scene this town offers. After all, that's what inspired Ci'Monique Green in her short story "113." Let yourself feel the anxiousness and anticipation of the open-mic in Carolyn Martin's story of a "minor poet" taking the stage at a bookstore and Elijah Cordero's "Calm Before the Slam."

Stroll the mossy cracked sidewalks and breathe in each of the four seasons through breathtaking imagery. Hopscotch through rain puddles with Ann Privateer, find a beacon of hope in a rainstorm with Matt Amott, long for the first glimpse of sun through the eyes of Nathan Tompkins, and surrender to a peachy sunset in July with Tricia Knoll. You might even find beauty and inner strength, as Denise Buschmann did, recalling the eruption of Mount. St. Helens.

Portland is a city rich in tradition and proud of its river heritage. Michael

Shay beautifully illustrates its history in both of his poems, as does Simon del Valle in his "Rivered Cliffs." It's a wonderful city to call home or simply pay a visit. DE Navarro's "Rite of Passage" recounts his time spent in this city, while Jenean McBrearty echoes that sentiment in her spiritual story.

Sure, it rains here – a lot. But, once the sun appears, so do a myriad of farmers markets, evident in the works of Justin W. Price and Sharon Lask Munson, who both pay homage to the Saturday open-air markets, celebrating home-grown delights and offerings from talented local artisans.

So what makes this place so weird? Well, I'm sure if you asked 100 people you'd get 100 different answers. So instead, I'll let the poet known as "M" describe "An Average Afternoon" and direct you to Steve Williams' tale about an orangutan named Ellie. Feel free to stop along the way to "scrawl some funky Tex-Mex" with Michael Berton.

Did you know that Portland has more strip clubs per capita than any other American city? Well, that fun fact didn't get past our poets either, as illustrated in Luke Warm Water's poem about Dino's strip club and mine about a "girl and a pole."

And to complete the cornucopia of weirdness, check out the new cult anthem, "Keep Portland Weird" by John & Mary Massimilla, and enjoy Susan Vespoli's double-dactyl poem which so eloquently and briefly illustrates the quirkiness of P-town.

We invite you to peruse these pages of poetry and short-stories. Pop open a bottle of micro-brew, join a band, start a compost meet-up group and fall in love with Portland. We sure did! And in the words of Brenda Taulbee, "we wish you were here."

~Shawn Aveningo

Weird Portland

Rosiest posiest
Portland inhabitants,
trash-sorting eco-friends,
brewers of beer.

Bridge-walking bicyclists,
environmentalists,
hyper-recyclers and
proud to be weird.

The Slant of Slate

Rooftops and sidewalks, slabs
of gray slate, memorized
walking to school, skates
humming, hopscotch
or step on a crack and you
break your mother's back,
walking backwards, giant
steps, baby steps playing
Mother May I or Jacks.
Steps stepping up, down,

dancing, running, tripping.
Rain turns slate ebony. Rooftops
sparkle on the horizon. I draw
with chalk on slabs of slate, grow
to teach children at a blackboard.
Slabs chiseled to fit, some split
apart, others last eons, side-walks
replaced with grass or cement,
laced into a new day, technology
casting different shadows.

The Helper in the Capitol Hill Library

His thin back is bent. He's balding.
What little hair he has frizzles.
He often wears a long gray cardigan.
He is not in charge here.

Recent automations do not prevent him from pushing carts,
swiping undisciplined cards in red lasers, pointing north
for read-to-me DVDs, south for mysteries, east for poetry,
west for picture books. The *New York Times Book Review*
stands behind his desk with Kindles.

Before Christmas I searched for a book on haiku
enlightenment, out of print, not in our catalog system,
more than seventy dollars on E-Bay for 175 leafy pages. He
led me through a sequence of screens. A national search.

I got an email alert after New Years. Come pick up a book
at my neighborhood library, just past Walgreens,
up hill from the middle school, past the mosque.
It's the 12th day of Christmas.

He turns to the inter-library loan shelf.
Distance: 2,426 miles from
Ohio Wesleyan University. No charge.

His eyebrows meet in the middle. He gets it,
how happy I am. Some other one,
the history librarian at Wesleyan,
donated this book to their shelves.
Librarians as elf.

> the wind turns over
> old leaves on the driveway
> my path to the fig tree

Average Afternoon, Portland

we are deep in the trench of January
winter has its hand
on our bundled up backs
rudely shoveling us like litter
down Glisan street
a man drives a cherry red Chevy 4 X 4
in the opposite direction
payload maxed out with
ladders power saws paint cans drywall
windows rolled all the way down
sound system jacked all the way up
the monkey puppet on his left hand
is smiling
waving indiscriminately at everyone
lip-syncing Tom Jones
it's not unusual
to be loved by anyone
and just like in a movie
when the sad boy makes
the clutch free throw
even though it's hokey
we cheer

Northeast Portland (NEP)

Not far from the Willamette
Marine Dr. hugs the banks of the Columbia like a thirsty dog
Never quite reaching either the sea on one side
Or the mountains on the other
Only Lombard stretches across the river here
Each new crossing a small waterfall of names
Where metal cargo containers line the road
Stacks of Lego deliberately painted
Flat sun bleached colors
While giant backhoes and excavators pose
Like praying mantes
Behind the teeth of shiny wire fences

There Killingsworth
Pushes straight through rounded stones
Glacial orphans
A street of gray promises
That reaches Swan Island
Landfilled several wars ago
Now an island in name only
Ainsworth toddles along
A wide old lady always dressed
In her slight shabby Sunday best
Under a large green hat of trees a hundred years old
The wind ruffles Prescott jogging
Lanes left or right
Two on one side or another
Depending who speaks and how far the journey has been
While Alberta is overflowing
Bold type on any map
An old creek turned Arts District
Confined in steep banks
Too fast to swim anymore

And Sandy strolls its leisurely diagonal
Hitching one neighborhood to another
Devoid of crows and stop signs

Carrying this part of the city on its shoulders
Fremont courses up and over hills
Which were dark blue once
But have since lost their color
It too is now full of nostalgia
Separating the soft memories
Of farmland
From Klickitat and Knott
Protecting the blue shadows of Wisteria
Hiding under the hill
And the names of presidents
From the thieving winds of the Gorge
Stealing the weather as they pass underneath
Singing their song into all those streets
With a steady beat of numbers, of places and avenues
Whose soft alliteration is a pulse that never stops
The rising and falling pitch, the Doppler sounds of tires
As Broadway delivers into its rust red bridge
All that neighborhood
A long lost cousin who promises to visit
And winds up staying far too long.

Rivered Cliffs

frothy, oblong drops
drip, drop downward
shelves of sheer, slippery shale
wearing beaded veils of rainfall
fall, falling
like autumn falls
slow motion suspended
floating
coasting down
to the gray scaled ground
held fast, at long last
in gravity's vice grip grasp
still frames, shaken
by off cast rocks
a crack, smack, crash
strong as long drawn doses
so precocious, unabashed
paths get chosen, phases pass
if not for those in modes of glass
then oft for roses froze in casts
mock crest logos, inset class

Rite of Passage

Oregon the Ancient Forrestal,
Wizard of Nature and the Northwestern Wood,
Keeper of Portland: Gateway to River and Sea
With gnarly staff of tangled Douglas Fir
Beckoned for and summoned me.

Portland walled me up in her stone towers
Preaching on the corners, Prophets, screaming out,
"You are damned, all of you, condemned,
Everyone be damned for daring decadence."
But all I saw was the state of the beavers,
Streets like streams swollen and pooling
Everyone dammed and cozy in their homes.

Not a soul stirred, no monk or Western Meadowlark
Oblivious in their duties as if they heard nothing,
Saw nothing, felt nothing — the icons of nothingness
Still screaming "repent" above the din of city traffic
Ornaments adorning corners, accepted as integral to
The weird and the wonderful.

They speak out of the "O" in Portland, Portal of Sages
Gateway to environment, beauty beyond measure
Trees and mountains holding their gem gentle in hand
Where the words of the prophets are written all over
Cement walls, dividers, underpasses and overpasses,
Warning of impending doom — proud placards of
The weird and the wonderful.

The Ancient Keeper gave me a sprig of Oregon Grape
Said "Wave it, wave it in the faces of the prophets,
For the 'O' closes soon and they must return thither."
As I passed them in the streets I waved the sprig

"Hear ye prophets, the 'O' closes the 'O' closes soon."
And one by one they slipped away and disappeared
Into the thin shimmering air of the rippled orange sun.
Night fell off busses and the city took up a dance
Celebrating life in the fantastical firelight of
The weird and the wonderful.

Oregon gave me rite of passage to the ship
Out of the Portland Rivers onto the Western Sea.
The people bid me farewell with glasses raised
In the mirth of the blood of the grape made wine.
I sailed away from the old prophetic city low
The towers quickly sinking into the confluence so that
Only green mountains and blue skies remained —
And vivid memories of the Oregonian Guard
Keeping it weird and wonderful.

Bowline

I have only learned to tie
Two knots and one hitch
In my life
The overhand
Simple and direct
One end crossing over the other
Secure only when done in pairs
It becomes a square knot
Requiring sharp pointed objects
To separate one knowingly from the other

The cleat hitch joins
One completely different thing to another
Two winds and a pass through
A simple figure eight
An eye half closed
Above the other
Each tug serving only to tighten
The flipped loop
The rope almost breathing
In and out

And in a world
Where everything is as easily erasable
Like a bowline thrown back on a deck
The coiled rope
Marks a beginning
Tied firmly there
While the other end that flaps in the breeze
Or falls seemingly unconcerned
In the water

Until pulled taut
When it sings in the wind

After Saturday Market

I color-coordinate my vegetables
into bowls of unexpected shades and hues,

sight and taste mingle in a dance of colors
like blue flax and scarlet poppies

cresting along the highway,
tints of blush on the edge of a bend

bursting forth with honeyed pleasure.
Ruddy, sugar-coated beets

thick, smooth as velvet
spill into plum colored basins.

Crunchy pole-beans drowse in amber crocks.
Blood-red tomatoes

thickly sliced, show off on white bone china,
while tender young carrots idle in cobalt.

Plump corn on the cob, lightly steamed
waits impatiently for a light slathering

of sweet yellow butter.

Open Air Market on the First Day of Spring
~For Allen Ginsberg

When the sun comes out, so do we, Portlanders.

Like flannel bedecked bears, we hibernated in wooden caves, protected by naked trees lining streets mushy with leaves, with mud, with rain.

We emerge, squinting and somewhat shorn, with jeans hugging legs and the sun painting its glisten upon us.

To the open air west side market with our suddenly sexy lady, no longer hiding curls beneath a cotton hat, no longer hiding perfect breasts and perfect flesh beneath argyle and shapeless cotton. Both pierced and ink stained, we walk past pink and white cherry blossoms shedding buds in the clever breeze.

To the market:

Where we learn the benefits of homemade soaps, of crystal gazing, of all natural, MSG-free food seasonings, where we remind ourselves why we endured nine months of rain and gloom, and reacquaint ourselves with the aroma of patchouli, of clove cigarettes, of reefer, of cooking flesh, of naturally lacquered pine (carved and nailed into birdhouses and signs welcoming visitors).

Past the djembe surrounded by long hair and hacky sacks, past the orange robed Hire Krishnas passing out free hard backed books for a one time donation, past the churro vendor's deadly enticements, past the stained glass artisans, to the cubic zirconias — just as pretty and less messy than diamonds — where we try on sterling rings and compliment our awareness. Past dogs and their strained smiled caretakers, and we pretend that we're not cooler than they are.

But we know.

We're cooler than everyone.

Our tattoos, our funky hairdos, the obscure bands on our t shirts, the way we walk, our ironic mustaches, our cat's eyes.

We know.

All this is processed and consumed as we wait in line for gyros. We scoff at the Budweiser and drink our micro. We eat and drink in wrought iron chairs, baking in the sun, sprayed by fountains of cold recycled water, we gaze past to the Willamette, to the tug boats, to the kayaks, to the east side.

Let's Go Trippin'
~Quotes by KC

She only arrived
in the Northwest
a few months back.
Leaving the tropical
islands with
a broken suitcase
and a broken heart
from a cheating
scoundrel.

My request
for a date
denied
again and again.
She hated the cold,
suffered
homesick sadness
and insisted on
acquaintances
as long as the winter
rain drowned her soul.

Then I showed up
at her place
with
a heat lamp,
Dick Dale records
salt and
tequila,

margaritas
and
dancing

all afternoon
'til
the supplies
ran low.

I knew her
heart thawed
when
"for want
of salt,
she licked
my neck."

Memorial Day

The sun punches
through the threadbare residue
of the cumulus clouds.

A hazy veil of indigo sky
heralds the ordained
invasion of summer.

I watch through
the dark tinted windows
of Rocco's Pizza
and leer at the battalions
of horny women
as they march in formation
passed this littered intersection
of 10th and Burnside.

Their uniforms of skintight shorts,
and miniskirts,
unmask fresh shaved legs
that glint with perspiration.

Their tits, barely hidden
by bikini tops and low cut blouses,
jangle with each step
of their high heeled sandals.

The volunteers of this estrogen brigade
are flourishing fuchsias that aspire
to be harvested from the topsoil of their birth,
a hope aroused by the closing spring.

Wednesday Will End At Dino's Strip Club

As for me I wallow in my depression
not even any energy left for desperation
since I do not partake
in the warm embrace
of booze, chemicals
nor women of the night
even porn has lost its luster

Find myself alone all the time
no woman calls for a second date
tend to believe it just rests
on I'm too weird and ugly
maybe not so weird
maybe I tell the truth these days
no longer want to hide
behind the lies
maybe I am a lazy man
tired man, fat man
but got to be a better man

So I will find the corner booth
inside Dino's strip club again tonight
which reminds of an old VFW club or
classic dive bar
the place where strippers go
to take off their clothes
at the end of their careers or
when no other clubs will have them
wrinkles and fat
crappy attitudes
small smiles which lost meaning years ago
small corner stage as their final stop

I bring someone else's poetry books
my trusty Moleskin notebook
bank roll of $1 bills
order up the RC Cola
and wait for new poems to visit me
they usually don't
so I sit in pervert row attentive or
in the side booths with book reading
just as out of place
as a shabbily clothed wino
in the Multnomah County library
admiring a book of Van Gogh paintings

I belong here at Dino's
with the mostly over the hill and overweight
less desirable beauties

We have a common bond
we both perform for a crowd of few
we are no longer stars
never really were
just legends in our own mind
we just keep doing it
to a small crowd that applauds
out of polite conditioning
my poems, as are their naked bodies
are not valued by most

I
unloved by women!
feared by poets!
understand ugly
on the exterior and within
in the Rose City
where everyone is friendly
but nobody wants to be your friend
Portland damn it!
I love you

The only thing I love more
are the strippers at Dino's
may they never get
Cabaret, Gentleman's club types
the strippers at Dino's
are perfect

A Girl and a Pole in Stumptown

Body Glitter.
Cuban Heel Stockings.
Pasties applied
at the peak of perkiness.

Slip into a pair of lucite stilettos –
not quite the glass slippers of girlhood fantasy.
Prince Charming now a bouncer,
enforces the "watch, don't touch" rule.

And a pole, her steady partner each night,
anchors her erotic acrobatics,
provides center to tassels-a-spin,
never once asking for a cut of the dough.

Hippie Wrinkles

the hype
of the hip
city everyone wants
to live in a paradigm
during early evening
brewpub crawls
tugboat hops
circuiting crater
butt molds poems
into poses
trickery in drag
faux vogue in
rogue's clothes
hemp grass
medicine man
tai chi
reflection
over big pink
moon shine
where okie
mutant salmon
bounce bridges
rainbow youth tread
queer leaps
on bike seats
honk for
obnoxious
deadhead poets
panhandling sex
at orgasmic
open mic
on alphabet street
rate

Harmonica

At dusk, the river rushes
through Sellwood Park,
sweeps away fallen branches, broken limbs,
pays no heed to the bluster of March winds.

Beside the channel, two men settle on a cedar bench.
Stooped, heads down, absorbed in the moment
they stroke metal reeds along the length
of their small mouth organs.

Traffic from the highway filters through,
joins the easygoing strains of Moon River —
two drifters off to see the world,
the ageless two-part harmony welcomes night

the pitch, the chords, a little higher now
leaves the river laughing.

Mid-July Peaches
Portland, Oregon

Summer heats up
AC yanks down windows
on neighbors' cocktail hour
   spats and TV gunshots
the fourth's charred paper, wire fuses, and glitter
   litter bone-dry streets
pirate boats eavesdrop
on the riverfront blues festival

crow alarm at 5 am
used to be 4:30
daylight's shrinking
like cotton on a laundry line

people who hated rain
whine about brown lawns
storm center radio, between songs
of who did who wrong, predicts
        high-90s for ten days
hard to make news
out of consistent summer
killer heat waves, range fires,
and drought strangling this West
though someone may be climbing Mt. Hood,
last window of opportunity melting in alpenglow

Smog silver-hazes the horizon.
Thick day ends in a peach sunset
so wide you might sail away
on peach juice, an inversion's gift
of bloodstone silhouettes,
from the river's edge, high-rise
teeth of buildings and banks
shadowed in dense inner-city jams.

To Wesley, Panhandling on SW 6th & Harrison, Portland, Oregon

Remember the woman walking
down the street, pushing bills
toward your tattered smile?
A better day! you offered me.

Than what? I asked, summer
still innocent, the urge for coffee
picking up my pace.
Courthouse Square beats you up.
Here the sneers are safe.

I tried to shake your hand.
TB, you warned. *Exposed.*

You'll earn a room tonight,
I hope. A second thought.
At least a poem.

I Scrawled Some Funky Tex-Mex on Burnside

steppin'
step in
step into
a total
chingonometricos
tlaloc somersault
strollin' over bridges
backwards barking
borracho ballet
into a fareless
jive ass bass line
where rubbers
are stretched and frayed
while liquor reeks
outside soup kitchens
a dropsy on
rainbow runaways
is where I broke
my slow low
hipster lines
rolled some Chicanas
from Woodburn
funky on Burnside

puro squares
on Burnside
with my new
side burns
and rouge
dirty chiva
muffled my trumpet
placed the blues
on me

so i
crawled
payaso like
along the walk
talkin' up
a good night
with some drizzle
hit my stride
goosing my
sauve sax
sexy on Burnside

who's talkin'
who's talkin' Calo
on Burnside
pitchin' a stream
of consciousness
peyote tracking
sounds of faraway Aztlan
reverberate Burnside

te buscando
y que mas
you lookin'
in squareless
on bus twenty
tambien el quince
you lookin'
on Burnside
you pay me
to scrawl
straddle
stanza strut

blowin' your harmonica
swingin' your daddy
funky drunk
on Burnside

te buscando
you lookin'
to stroke
la raza
on Burnside
you play me
ladies
with a fright
dealers
with the might
gettin' bumped!
bumped! bumped!
on Burnside

mi amor
my muse
tells me when
poetry panhandles
well with nalgonometricos
mitote conniptions
exercising gestures
syllabic solicitations
walkin' words and deeds
up and down blocks
with a gimp
in my stride
humming a chrome
and metronome cadence
in funky time
and raw theatrics
you pay me
on your way out
off Burnside

Translations:
mitote - an Aztec dance, commotion
chingonometricos - a supreme bad-ass
nalgonometricos - maximum big butts
(the suffix, "metricos" is used to multiply/maximize on the root word)

The Calm Before The Slam

The brain teases ivory elegance
with growing pigments
of inspiration

A blank page

Ready to be shaped into glances of inquiry & wisps
of indignation as a veil of innuendo filters the light into shades
of hot pink and crimson

With shattered resignation the clique wades
into the pool of amplified muses

A blank page

Entices organically coded literature
from the spendthrift of aesthetics

To dare

To bare

To share

These dreams and visions with those that hunger
for inspiration

A Minor Poet Takes the Stage at an Independent Bookstore in Portland, Oregon

I ease toward the lectern,
the one that tilts unless cardboard
props the back right leg.

I forgot to check.
Too busy schmoozing with regulars
who traipse from site to site
and the host – proper, precise –
chancing an unknown.

I lean slightly right, stutter-step
a word or two, then settle down:
Thirty-seven years ... first book ...
compendium of memories.

The third-row woman nods a smile,
the fourth-row man a frown.
What draws them out? I wonder,
gaining voice. *What draws them in?*

I used to know.
When keynotes hit their mark in worlds
of business suits and strategies;
when I earned, We want you back,
celebrity was clear.

But here, in miles of time away
from mini-bars and turned-down sheets,
I'm not so sure metaphors motivate
or lines reshaped for twists of sound
net a response. Cost/benefit
analysis, I've told myself
a dozen times, does not apply.

Thirteen poems. At last.
Polite applause.

Never again! I chide myself –
stashing notes on *how's* and *why's* –
and plan to charge the center aisle
and flee into self-comforting.

That is, until the frowner clears a path
through comments quasi-hushed, unastute.
Two hands on the lectern,
he wants a copy of my book.

Barefoot

running through uncut grass, toes comb
puddles, mud oozes past each digit

barefoot speaking, confident
stepping up to the podium

where a hawk circles the night sky
and I with two nude feet itch

to be done, to relax, pointing
them up into infinity.

T-Shirts

I want to ask the knobby man
walking by the monkey house
with the 'Porn Star' t-shirt –
the man with shorts two sizes too large
billowing over white socks
and brown sandals,
what he wore yesterday.

I want to ask the screaming chimpanzees
throwing shit our direction
if they were ever in one of his movies.

I want to ask the man with wire rim glasses
poking out from under his corduroy cap
walking silently through the innumerable
"Oh my Gods" and the occasional
"I'd ask for my money back,"
If we're on Candid Camera.

It never occurs to me to ask if he has any kids,
where his hometown might be,
or if he can tell me his real name.

I want to ask the porn star
outside the orangutan viewing area
if he knows Ellie like I know Ellie.
She is sitting patiently inside, intent on watching him
watch her. She motions him closer, yawns,
then waves him aside like she's ready
for the next page of the picture book
I held out for her only yesterday.

Now, her eyes fixed on the shirts

in a congress of plump high schoolers
that announce "Pleased to eat you."
and "Tourist from 2512."

I want to ask Ellie if she can read.

I wonder if I stink. I hope so ... The way my t-shirt is sticking to my bra-less back and a palpable plume of something inordinate is wafting from my scalp, I wouldn't be surprised. As I press my forehead against the murky window, taking in the world coming to the stop of a new beginning before me, I scratch the wriggling itchiness in my hair and smile – vindicated.

I finally grappled free from the illusion I was forced to live.

My dad, Dr. Gunther Balacuit, is a "to die for" plastic surgeon to the stars, the rich, and the hopelessly insecure in Beverly Hills, and I am his beloved princess daughter. Out of all his five other children from his four previous wives, I'm the only girl – and truly, for-really, the only one he loves. When he married my mom (his repeat rhinoplasty patient), Alexis, twenty years ago and brought me home from the hospital a month later, he somehow discovered his life's mission: to turn his daughter into Tinsel Town royalty.

I had servants standing watch over my crib, and butt-wipers for my butt-wipers for every suffocating minute I lived in our Brentwood mansion. It was extreme, pathological, and maddening. So, two nights ago I threw a pair of jeans and a clump of underwear into my backpack and bypassed the security system to escape to freedom. With $300 in my wallet, I left my $2000 monthly allowance and trust fund behind ... along with all other pretentious booty – like a hair brush, toothpaste, or deodorant.

I am not a princess. And as I flush my face deeper against the vibrant new world taking shape through the window, I know the adventure I've been starving for is waiting for me in this wonderfully weird city.

The Amtrak slows to a stop at the Portland station at exactly 3:32 on a steamy, summer afternoon. After the 30-hour ride from LA, the herd of passengers on the funky-smelling vessel rise up around me, stretching out cricked necks and kneading reddened eyes. While we gather our stuff and move to the aisle to dismount the train, I grin and nod at the eclectic mix of strange peeps thronging me.

I see guitars on the backs of an über-pierced pack of guys rockin' dreadlocked beards. Spilling from the upper deck, I'm almost stampeded by five boisterous chicks, including a sassy fat girl in ripped fishnets with a chartreuse pompadour. I let them barrel past me and enter the station, feeling a certain euphoria as we all prick the same force field.

The second my feet hit the grimy ground of my new home, I realize the exciting dramatics of what I've just done. My family doesn't know where I am. I'm a thousand miles away from everything familiar. I don't know one soul in Portland. And I only have $167 left.

This kind of recklessness can only lead to bliss.

I smile against the wild P-Town energy surrounding me, compelled to do what I've been dreaming of. I walk over to a sticky wooden bench, edging beside a homeless man taking a midday snooze. From my backpack, I pull out a pen and tablet, barely letting them consummate before the words start raging:

> *POETLAND*
>
> *Drown my crown*
> *In your sea*
> *Of mystery*
>
> *Bathe my eyes*
> *With your*
> *Empty luxury*
>
> *Be my bliss ...*
> *Abduct my kiss*
>
> *Fill my frenzied hand*
> *Oh, strange Portland*

Something my dad never understood about me is that I'm a poet. I wasn't born to don a tiara – I was created to pen odd obscurity. I've been dying for this day to come when I could actually sit in this quirky place and write about it. And whatever it takes, I'm gonna experience something life-changing on my first night in Portland.

"Hey, whassup? What's your name?"

The electric voice tumbles down on me from an unexpected place: the lips of a guy suddenly standing six inches in front of me.

My eyes orbit as I look up at him. "Oh. Hi. Camilla ..."
"Mmm, Camilla. That's pretty." He smiles mysteriously, glowing with a cute cosmic face I can't tell is real or an apparition. "Listen ... I was on the train with you from LA. I was hoping I could show you around once we got here."

I hold his gaze, pondering. "How did you ...?"

"I could tell you weren't from here. And I want you to do Portland the right way." His look is celestially disarming. Thrilling.

With the cantankerous sounds of the train station lulling into a drowned hum in my ears, I feel something epic abiding in his invitation.

So I accept.

"Okay. Yeah, definitely." I smile huge at the bizarre stranger.

"Cool ..." He responds, gleaming. "If you're down, can I take you by my place first? I wanna show you something."

I sense the words I just set to flight on my tablet birthing through the moment. I'm ready to mount wings and fly anywhere. "Alright ... Sounds cool. Where is it?"

My willingness inches him closer to me. He reaches down to diddle my fingers with a beguiling touch that fizzles my insides.

"Right over the bridge. The Jupiter. Room 113."

Hope Sandoval Sings My Blues

It started raining
as she and I sat
in the car
near Union Station.
Mazzy Star played
on the radio
while she told me
I wasn't the one
she loved.

Exiting the vehicle
into the storm,
an outbound
whistle
sounds-

a beacon
for the
wayward
and
broken-hearted.

Tequila Bones

I told you I loved you
before I knew it was true.
That summer smelled
like cigarettes and cheap beer,
like sweat and fear and lonely.
I had been drunk
every day for six months
the night we strapped
your mattress to a jeep.
That night you asked to sleep
in my bed, standing
in my doorway.
You were
sad and lovely
in a way that made me
want to invent new words.

Last winter
through a kitchen window
that would never be ours
you showed me the place
you used to smoked cigarettes
in your underwear.
Sometimes
late at night I smoke
cigarettes on my roof
feeling lonely for that girl I never knew.
I want to tell her everything will be fine.
I want to believe everything will be fine.

Two nights ago
the lights stretched below us,
slow cars like sticky platelets

gliding through the city's veins.
We seared solar flares into our lungs
let smoke stun the swarm of truths
trapped beneath our tongues.
I didn't mean to laugh
but we're constantly
halfway between
tragedy and comedy.

Yesterday.
You held me like a baby
while I wept, knees to chest,
my face pressed
into the crease of your neck.
You asked me why I'll always choose the rain
and I can't explain except
I keep hoping it will help me
appreciate the sun.

When I was young
I slept with my feet uncovered
so I could run through my dreams.
I'd cling to my bedpost so
I never lost my way back.
Now I sleep
holding onto the pieces of myself
I'm most afraid of losing,
dig fingertips into my own ribs
as if I could knit myself back together.
You told me you'll always be there
when I need to find my way back.
But you are not mine to look for anymore.

Tomorrow.
I will leave this town.
And when the plane banks low
over the snow covered peak

of Mount Hood
I won't remember the way
your forehead tastes
every time I'm kissing you
goodbye.

Imagine me somewhere.
Imagine me peaceful.
Don't check in.
I don't want to disappoint you again.
I might call you home
and you call me best friend
but in the end they're just different words
for "never."

Tomorrow.
I'll go back to the places
that gravity feels lightest.
I'll remember how to sleep again,
remember dreams without you in them.
I used to laugh
when you talked about
going back to Real Life
like somehow we could slip
in and out of reality
the way you put on a winter jacket
to survive the worst of the cold.

I'm not laughing anymore.

Last year
in the winter tomb of your bedroom
you asked what I want to be
when I Grow Up, and I'm sorry I lied
when I laughed and said "Alive."

See, I want to be a star.

Or the idea of a star;
something you can wish on.
A spinning supernova
that implodes far away
and in its ultimate act
of self-destruction
finally attains beauty.

Dance Beneath Streetlights

We disembark the Portland Spirit
crash half drunk feet up the gangway,
your fingers woven into mine,
your eyes still glow from candlelight,
mouth still savours two bottles of wine.

You sit down on a green park bench,
beads of rain still clot it's painted surface.
I reach down, grab your right hand,
and lift you from your iron seat.

I shroud your neck with my arms,
smell aromatic traces of merlot
upon your breath as I sing
for your ears alone, my audience of one.
We slow dance beneath two yellow streetlights
upon the spring drizzle damp sidewalk.

Since then, you gave me a daughter.
Since then, I gave you my last name.
Since then, our lips tasted goodbye.
Since then, we took off our rings ....

One day, my tattooed arms will drape another
as my whispered song seeps into her ears
and we sway beneath two cold yellow streetlights
upon a drenched sidewalk in Waterfront Park.

Away From Portland, September 1980

I remember the day we rented
the house that reeked of dog piss
that I'd pled, "No, let's not."
We shared it with two Christian girls,
one whose heart you broke.

I remember we borrowed
furniture from someone you chatted up
at the hardware store,
her kindness and generosity, touching.
"I'm not using it," she said.
"Meet me at my storage locker."

I remember you toweling off
after your shower,
your body taunt, dark, tall
     as a Hollywood god's

and catching
your self-satisfied glimpse
     in the mirror —
that's when I knew.
My wrenching gut validated
what our vows meant
to you.

I remember unbridled tears flowing,
eyes burning, the odor of sulfur lingering
long in swollen nostrils,
glass in my chest,

and externals coated with gray volcanic-ash smut
like breaded meat,

after cleaning windows
to make the money
to get back home
to the East Coast.

I remember two weeks later
rubbernecking from the air,
Mt. St. Helens,
still spitting fire, emitting poisons,
destroying peace and sanctity —
like the turmoil inside me.

But, most of all,
I try not to remember
you at the screen door, wearing
a vacant little smile, waving
like a three year old
as I walked out that morning
on my way to the airport
away from Portland
away from you.

Wish You Were Here

the city
is wearing
your eye color again
inappropriate
like a christmas cardigan

in july. stifling.

when the man on the corner
ask for change
i describe the
inside of your elbow —

crisscrossed highways
of anatomy, how you always
stretched the boundaries
of your skin.

i promise the sidewalk
to leave unlucky pennies
where they lie if its cracks
will stop resembling
your hands. life lines
like water spilling to the
edge of each palm.

i don't know how to talk
about your kneecaps,
the gravity of your slapdash mouth.
your two eyes looking at her
like water. my two eyes
looking at you the same;

or your name
under my tongue. the
biggest lie i ever told.

A Visit to Portland

> *On the banks of the Willamette, as it flows into the sea,*
> *there's a lovely, lovely city that belongs to you and me.*
> *It's the City of the roses, the home of royalty,*
> *it's Portland my home town.*

"Really?"

"Sung to the tune of The Battle Hymn of the Republic. I swear to God, we sang it in Miss. Patterson's 3rd Grade class. She was black. In 1956 it said a lot about Portland that she taught in a mostly white school, albeit in the projects."

"Who thought that up, do you think?"

"I think the projects were old military housing."

"I meant, who do you think wrote the lyrics?"

"Someone who'd been to the rose gardens near the amphitheater. Portland's almost as dreary as Seattle. Gray and misty. The cemeteries look like the ones in English vampire movies."

My therapist checked her notes. "Maybe that's where your chronic depression started."

"Maybe. Childhood environments cast the character." College educated clients with literary pretensions must suck. Andrea Neatly—certainly living up to her name if not her potential—probably wasn't prepared for a gospel song response to the typical psychologist's opening salvo: So, tell me about your childhood. She wore her Nice N' Easy sable brown hair pulled back off of her perfectly shaped head, and knotted it at her nape. It looked like a muffin attached to her neck. Are there vampires who sink their fangs into muffins?

Andrea returned to her notes. "You wrote here that you grew up in San Diego."

"Mother liked to sunbathe in the nude." She didn't. She made my sister and me wear girdles when we were ten, then handed us over to the nuns who made us wear hair-shirts and shackles.

Andrea finally smiled a 'professional distance' smile. Strained. Like someone offered her a raw oyster on a half shell and she said she was allergic to shell fish. "Is that true, Gisele?"

"Before we left Portland to get away from my father and his whiskey-drinking whore, Mother took us to see the Garden of Our Sorrowful Mother. She parked her red '41 Chevy coupe at the bottom of a small mountain and we rode a huge elevator to the top. I've been afraid of anything that resembles a silver tube ever since. Air planes, ball point pens, pewter spoons. The statuary in the garden is just as frightening. All white marble holy people condemned to remain in suffering poses until the marble rots. Okay, until the wind beats it into sand. Which, if it wasn't for the bushes and trees, might be half the time of regular marble disintegration. Mother saw the dew still on the leaves at noon and said she needed to move where it was warm."

"Did you miss your friends when she took you to San Diego?"

Andrea was trying to build empathy, but the question was falsely premised on the assumption I had friends. A better question would have been, did I miss my father. "I missed my dog." We lived on St. Helen's Road. Daddy worked at the steel mill near the big oil storage tanks. One of them blew up, and he rushed home, piled us in the car and speeded up the hill passed the Montgomery Ward, passed the big Smokey the Bear that stood outside the Forestry Department's log cabin. I could see the thick black smoke billowing up like a mushroom cloud over the valley. It must have reminded Daddy of Korea.

"Have you ever been back?"

"Only when I talk to counselors." Twice. Once for a job interview and once on the way to Washington. I drove over to St. Helen's Road, but left because everything was gone except for the log cabin. Government buildings last as long as marble.

Andrea closed her notebook. Quietly. In one smooth motion, without fuss or flourish. She'd write a report for my lawyer detailing my disability adjustment difficulty stemming from a suspected pre-existing personality disorder. Undeniable just the same.

Hell yes, I'm screwed up. I have post-polio syndrome. In 1956, the first polio vaccine was tested on elementary school children in Portland. I waited in line, having to pee as I neared the table where sharp silver tubes were stabbed into our skinny arms. After parental consent forms were double-checked. I had to stay home for a few days because of a "mild reaction" at the injection site. A mild but malignant I'll-get'cha-in-forty-years reaction, Mr. Salk. Childhood environments can cripple the best of us.

Keep Portland Weird
(song lyrics)

People walkin' down the street.

They don't care what you think.

Long hair. Bus Fare.

And you see them Everywhere!

Crazy Dress. Cost less.

Not here to impress.

Let's just keep

  Let's just keep

    Let's just keep

      Portland ... WEIRD!

Food carts, dive bars,

Strange sights fill the night.

Rip City. Hawthorne Street.

Feel the beat beneath your feet.

Tye-dye. Micro brews

In the park. Play the blues.

Let's just keep

  Let's just keep

    Let's just keep

      Portland ... WEIRD!

Why ... Why ...Why ...

  Would you ever move away from here?

Just believe. Life's so free,

I wanna stay here end … less … ly.
Everybody's in a band.
Go online. Become their fan.
Open mics. Take your pick.
Show up late. Play your licks.
Land a gig. Play for tips.
Rock the house. You won't get rich.

Let's just keep
   Let's just keep
      Let's just keep
         Portland … WEIRD!

Ha, ha, ha … He, he, he …
   … Ho, ho, ho … Ha, ha, ha …

Mud puddles. Green grass.
Share the road. Pedal your ass.
Strip clubs. Organic food.
Old Hippies. Get tattooed.
Get your ya-ya's out of here.
Come to stay. Have no fear.

Let's just keep
   Let's just keep
      Let's just keep
         Portland … WEIRD!

St Johns. Mt Tabor.
Old Town. Taste the vapor.
See the doc. Get your card.
It's not hard. Cook the lard.

Screen the green. Bring to boil.
Now it's time. Extract the oil.

Let's just keep
  Let's just keep
    Let's just keep
      Portland ... WEIRD!

Ha, ha, ha ... He, he, he ...
  ... Ho, ho, ho ... Ha, ha, ha ...

Let's just keep
  Let's just keep
    Let's just keep
      Portland ... WEIRD!

* as performed by local Portland band, MJ12

Matt Amott is a poet, photographer, a wanderer and charter member of the Pacific Vagabonds. As a co-founder of Six Ft. Swells Poetry Press, most of his research and work for the press is done "in the field." His ramblings tend to favor the short poem due to the lack of space on the cocktail napkin. He has been published in numerous journals and reviews, and his poems have been selected for the Poems-For-All Series in Sacramento and San Diego. He has read his work on KVMR (Nevada City, CA), KFOK (Lake Tahoe, CA), KUSF (SF State College Radio), as well as KBOO (Portland, OR). Always one to keep on the move, Matt has called Portland his home 3 times over the last 20 years but he continues to leave broken hearts and free mini chap books in bars and pubs along the West Coast. Matt and Six Ft. Swells Press can be found at afterhourspoetry.com.

Shawn Aveningo is a globally published, award-winning poet who can't stand the taste of coconut, eats pistachios daily and loves shoes....especially red ones! She believes poetry, especially when read aloud, is the perfect literary art form for today's fast-paced world due to its power to stir emotion in less than two minutes. Shawn's poetry has appeared in over 60 literary journals, anthologies and e-zines and she has authored 4 solo collections. She's given birth on two continents, and her three children make her an extremely proud "mama bear". She shares the creative life and business with her best friend & soul-mate, and they have recently made Portland, Oregon their home. (redshoepoet.com)

Michael Berton is an educator, percussionist and world traveler. Poems have appeared in *Perfume River Poetry Review, Indefinite Space, The Ambush Review, Yellow Medicine Review, Blaze VOX, Otoliths, Gertrude, And/Or, Faultlines Poetry, Pacific Review, Volt, The Blinking Cursor, Night Bomb Review, Do Hookers Kiss?, REM Magazine, Sin Fronteras Journal, Fireweed, The Cracked Mirror* and others. His first collection of poems, *Man! You Script The Mic.* (New Mitote Press) came out in 2013. (tzintzuntzan000@gmail.com)

Denise Buschmann is an herb gardener, her schnauzers' human, and Assistant Editor of two Northwest Indiana magazines. She erratically coordinates the Indiana chapter of Editorial Freelancers Association (EFA).

Her poetry has been published by Chicago Poetry Press in *Journal of Modern Poetry* 15 & 17, *Poetry Garden* 8, is included in *Bridge of Fates* anthology, and received Honorable Mention in the Contemporary American Poetry Prize (June, 2014). She also writes book reviews for *Retirement Living Magazine*.

Elijah Cordero has been in Portland for over 10 years – living, loving and surviving. He originally wrote poetry and performed spoken word in California. He was even in a variety show at the Ice House Annex in Pasadena for about 6 months. He has been published once in an old glossy local zine distributed in the Pearl District called *Scene Magazine* (no longer in publication). He has 3 kids and shares custody with their Mom.

Ci'Monique Green is the Beverly Hills Book Award-winning author of two novels, *Love Is As Strong As Death* and *Desperate Hope Arise*, as well as the self-illustrated children's poetry book, *Have You Ever Tasted a Rainbow?* Ci'Monique's riveting poem, "Sorry To Interrupt", was recently published in the anthology, *The Black Rose of Winter*. The native Seattleite and Los Angeles transplant is also an online columnist for Examiner.com, an artist, photographer, kick boxer, ice cream and pizza-lover, and the quirky blogger of three popular blogs: Owl In Pants, Jehovah's Poet, and What's Your Weird Food? (cimoniquegreen.com)

Tricia Knoll is a Portland, Oregon poet. Her poems and haiku appear in many journals and several anthologies – including recently *CALYX*, *Glass*, *Windfall*, *VoiceCatcher* and *The New Verse News*. Her chapbook *Urban Wild* is available from Finishing Line Press, Amazon and Annie Bloom's Books in Portland. She is a Master Gardener – trying to restore singing tree frogs to her neighborhood by introducing them to her native garden. Her frequent dance partner is a hula hoop. Her dog rings Turkish goat bells to be let in. (triciaknoll.com)

M is a Person. Poet. Performer. Sometimes even in that order.

Carolyn Martin is blissfully retired in Clackamas, OR, where she gardens, writes and plays with creative colleagues. Currently, she is president of the board of VoiceCatcher, a nonprofit that connects women writers and artists in greater Portland, OR / Vancouver, WA. (www.voicecatcher.org). Her work has appeared in publications such as *Stirring*, *5/Quarterly*, *Becoming:*

What Makes a Woman, *Persimmon Tree*, and the *Naugatuck River Review*. Carolyn's worst grades in elementary school were in Composition, and the only poem she wrote in high school was described as "extremely maudlin." Consequently, she remains confused by the fact that she continues to write. (portlandpoet@gmail.com)

Jenean McBrearty is a retired teacher who lives in Kentucky, takes classes at EKU, drinks tea, and pretends she's a princess. Or, on a cloudy day, Norma Desmond. Her fiction, photographs, and poetry have been published in many journals and anthologies. Her novel, *The 9th Circle*, was published by Barbarian Books. Her YA novels, *Rapahel Redcloak* and *Retrolands*, are serialized on *Jukepop*. (Jenean-McBrearty.com)

MJ12 is the classic rock band who shares their name with the US Government's "Above Top Secret" entity in charge of "Reverse Engineering UFO/Alien Technology". The band's founding members, Mary and John Massimilla, have been composing music and performing together since 1995. John is an accomplished, self-taught, lead guitar player from Portland, Oregon, who has created his own electrifying sound. Mary was raised in Los Angeles in a show-business family; her dad encouraged her to sing and perform with him at the tender age of six. Together John and Mary have composed a myriad of songs, including the new cult favorite *Keeping Portland Weird*. They have recently added drummer, Robert Sanders, to the mix and are actively auditioning bass players to round out the group's sound to share their music on the local stages of Portland and beyond.

Sharon Lask Munson lives and writes in Eugene, Oregon. She knows every curve and exit along I-5, taking her to Portland regularly. Her poetry has been published in many journals and anthologies, including poems forthcoming in *River of Earth and Sky*, *Edge*, *Indiana River Review*, *Windfall*, and *Wine, Cheese and Chocolate*. She is the author of the chapbook, *Stillness Settles Down the Lane* (Uttered Chaos Press, 2010) and a full-length book of poems, *That Certain Blue* (Blue Light Press, 2011). Her upcoming collection, *Braiding Lives*, a finalist in the 2014 Poetica Publishing chapbook contest, will be released in the fall. (sharonlaskmunson.com)

DE Navarro, born in Newport, Rhode Island, grew up in inner city Chicago, then rural Crown Point, Indiana and finally suburban Munster,

Indiana until he went to college. His love of poetry and writing began at age eight and in 1980 he was a featured poet in the Purdue Exponent. Since then his work has appeared in various magazines, publications, literary journals, anthologies, and online. He compiled and produced the poetry anthology, *Between Life and Language* in 2009, and *Dare to Soar in* 2013, a diverse collection of his own poems. DE lives in the greater Los Angeles area. (www.de-navarro.com)

Justin W. Price is the author of the poetry collection, *Digging to China*, published by Sweatshoppe Publications in 2013. He has lived in the Portland metro area for most of his life. His work has been published in many publications, including *eFiction*, *The Rusty Nail*, *The Hellroaring Review*, *The Bellwether Review*, *Page and Spine*, *Literary Juice* and *Best New Writing* (2014). When he's not writing poetry, stories or novels, he can be found working at Whole Foods, playing with his dogs and performing karaoke with his wife Andrea.

Ann Privateer was born in Cleveland, Ohio, but Los Angeles, California stole her heart. She moved there, completed college, married and moved north to raise a family. Ann retired from teaching and spends some of the year in Paris, France with family. Her poems have appeared in *Manzanita*, *Poetry Now*, *Tapestries*, *Entering*, and *Tiger Eyes*, to name a few. Photography and painting are recent interests. Some of her photos have appeared in *Rattlesnake Review*, *Medusa's Kitchen*, and one recently took a prize in the City of Davis Photography Contest, 2013. Her painting "Tooling" won best of show in the 2012 County Fair.

Robert R. Sanders has won over three dozen international awards in creative design, animation, and photography. He was nominated for an Emmy for *Fire Mountain*, a news documentary detailing the eruption of Mount. St. Helens and the Pacific Ring of Fire. Robert's work spans half a century of creative development through an analog and digital journey, where he is always in the front of the lunatic mass, always leading. He's a teacher to thousands of aspiring artists, while always remaining a student of the light. As a successful commercial photographer, author, and mentor, his work is sometimes dramatic, sometimes clever, at times controversial, but always sensually intriguing and impacting. (www.RobertSandersPhoto.com)

Michael Shay was born in Germany, grew up in Chicago and studied at both the Undergraduate and Graduate Iowa Writers' Workshop in poetry, He received a Master of Creative Arts in Interdisciplinary and Experimental Art from San Francisco State (CEIA) and makes his living as a commercial photographer in Portland, OR. Since he started writing again after a 15 year hiatus, he has been a contributing editor to *The Alberta St. Anthology* (Volumes I and II) and has had work appear in *The Cape Rock, Flyway, Nimrod International Journal of the Arts, Lullwater Review, The South Carolina Review* and *Rhino,* among others.

Brenda Taulbee first read poetry publicly in September 2012 with the Stone Soup Reading series. Before that, her cat, Murphy's Law, served as her primary audience. She self-published her first chapbook, *Dances with Bears ... And Other Ways to Lose a Limb* in June 2013. Her work has been accepted for publication in several online and literary magazines, including the *Gobshite Quarterly, The Inflectionist Review,* and *INK NOISE QUARTERLY.* The pinnacle of her poetic career was petting Andrea Gibson's dog, Squash.

Nathan Tompkins is a poet and photographer living, working, writing and generally goofing off in the Portland area. He has been published in *Alchemy, The Bellwether Review, Ghost Town Anthology II,* as well as two chapbooks *Junk Mail of the Heart* and *The Dog Stops Here.* His favorite things to do when he's not writing, shooting, or working is to drink beer and whiskey, irritate people and ogle pretty women.

Simon del Valle was born and raised in the college town of San Luis Obispo, CA. He attended the University of Oregon for a quarter before realizing that his most innate passion laid not in academia, but in words and music. After returning to his 'tierra natal' and completing a degree in Audio Technology at Cuesta College, he moved to Portland to pursue poetry. During his time there, he became close friends with the city's 'unofficial poet laureate' and author of *Mala Noche,* Walt Curtis. They co-host *Readaround – Spoken Words from Wherever,* Thursdays at 5pm on kpsu.org. Simon lived the last half year in New Orleans, where he bar tended on Bourbon St. and was published by Portals Press in an anthology of the oldest poetry reading in North America called *Maple Leaf Rag.* (simondicedelvalle@gmail.com)

Susan Vespoli lives mainly in Phoenix, AZ but sometimes in Prescott, with her partner and dogs. She fell in love with Portland when visiting, which inspired her poem. She is a teacher, poet, and born-again-bicyclist. Her work has been published in various journals and anthologies including *OVS Magazine*, *Verse Wisconsin*, *Merge*, and *The New Verse News*, and she was nominated for a Pushcart Prize.

Luke Warm Water resided in Portland from 2000 to 2003. His submitted poem first appeared in *John Wayne Shot Me* (2000). Dino's changed its name and is currently known as the Hawthorne Strip.

Steve Williams lives and works in Portland with a lovely woman who writes and edits much better than him, but refuses to admit it. Together, they host the Figures of Speech reading series at In Other Words feminist community center, are co-chairs of the Portland Unit of the Oregon Poetry Association, and attend as many poetry events as they can get to. Steve likes to support online journals and thus has most of his work in places like *Stirring*, *The Rose and Thorn*, *Word Riot* and other on-line journals.

Acknowledgments

"Let's Go Trippin'" and "Hope Sandoval Sings My Blues" by Matt Amott first appeared in *The Coast Is Clear* (Six Ft. Swells Press, 2012)

"To Wesley, Panhandling on SW 6th and Harrison, Portland, Oregon " by Carolyn Martin first appeared in *Elohi Gadugi* (Summer Issue, 2012)

"Wednesday Will End At Dino's Strip Club" by Luke Warm Water first appeared in *John Wayne Shot Me* (Chapbook, 2000)

As you enjoy these poems and stories, you may notice unique spelling, irregular punctuation (or lack there of), as well as stylized format and grammar choices in the text of the author's individual works. We at The Poetry Box™ strongly believe in artistic integrity and poetic expression, and therefore, did not make any changes or corrections without first consulting the authors. We urge our readers to enjoy not only the words written on the page, but also the meaning expressed by our authors in their unique, and sometimes quirky, choices in presenting their poems and stories to the audience.

The Poetry Box™ was founded in 2011 by Shawn Aveningo and Robert R. Sanders, who whole-heartedly believe that every day spent with the people you love, doing what you love, is a moment in life worth celebrating.

It all started out as a way to help people memorialize the special milestones in their lives, by creating custom poems with photographic artwork for anniversaries, birthdays, holidays and other special occasions. In order to accommodate a variety of budgets and tastes, they created a line of ready-made poetic artwork and notecard sets as part of the online Gift Shoppe. And for those who aren't necessarily looking for "poetry" themed gifts, they began offering Photo Art featuring some of Robert's fine art photography.

Robert and Shawn expanded on their shared passion for creating poetry and art, with the introduction of Poetry Box Publishing. Their debut publication, *Verse on the Vine – A Celebration of Community, Poetry, Art & Wine*, was an anthology featuring poets & performers who graced the stage of their acclaimed Verse on the Vine™ poetry series, which ran for two years in Folsom, CA.

The book you now hold in your hands, *Keeping It Weird*, is a true labor of love as Robert and Shawn embrace Portland as their new homestead and plan on continuing to celebrate the talents of their fellow artisans and writers. In addition to publishing two themed anthologies per year, The Poetry Box™ will soon offer their professional book design, graphic and publishing services to poets looking to publish their own collections and authors looking to publish novels.

And as always, The Poetry Box™ continues its pledge to give back to their community. Each month a portion of all sales will benefit a different charity. For a complete list of the charities currently supported, check out the Giving Back page on their website.

For more information, feel free to visit www.thePoetryBox.com or email Shawn@thePoetryBox.com.

Order Form

Need more copies for friends and family? No problem. We've got you covered with two convenient ways to order:

1. Go to our website at www.thePoetryBox.com and click on Bookstore.

OR

2. Fill out the order form below and email it to Shawn@thePoetryBox.com or mail it to The Poetry Box, 2228 NW 159th Pl, Beaverton, OR 97006.

Name: _____

Shipping Address: _____

_____

Phone Number: (_____)_____

Email Address: _____ @ _____

Payment Method: __ Cash __Check __ Paypal Invoice __ Credit Card

Credit Card #: _____ _____ _____ _____ CCV Code: _____

Expiration Date: _____ Signature: _____

Keeping It Weird - # of Copies: _____

x $12.00: _____

Plus Shipping & Handling: _____
($2 per book, or $5.95 for 3 or more books)

Order Total: _____

Thank You

Made in the USA
San Bernardino, CA
14 December 2014